The Nativity Of Jesus

CHRISTMAS PLAY WRITTEN BY

FATHER CHESTER FABISIAK, S.J.

The Nativity of Jesus
© 2018 Dr. Danuta B. Fabisiak. All rights reserved.

Published in the USA

Printed in the United States of America
ISBN: 978-1981192-0-7

Interior book design by Darlene Swanson • www.van-garde.com

May this Christmas story touch hearts,

renew joyful spirits, and

spread love and good cheer.

The Nativity of Jesus was written by my beloved uncle,
Father Chester Fabisiak, SJ

Submitted in loving memory by a forever grateful niece,
Dr. Danuta B. Fabisiak

Contents

Introduction

SMALL GIRL: I am very little, but I wish to present to you the
lovely story of:

How on a silent night a baby boy named Jesus came,
And the heavenly angels sang for joy.
How the star shown over the stable
So the shepherds were able to find the child
As he lay on the sweet-smelling hay.

How wonderful it must have been when the beasts,
The shepherds and the kings came to greet
The little baby in the manger.

How tender is the story of the first Christmas night,
Shepherds in a lonely field, bathed in heaven's light.

We learn humility; the greatness of simple things again,
The Christmas story touches our hearts and renews our spirit.
If we could live each day with love in our midst,
Peace among all nations indeed would exist.

Tonight we have come, as we do every year
To tell you of the first Christmas of love and good cheer.

We trust you will listen with hearts and with souls
To hear of the Christ child;
The story that never grows old.

ACT I

ACT I

Scene I. The Devil's Council.

A dark room, like a cave. Dry trees: some standing, some sitting, others moving.

RICK: (After a short silence.) Have you lost your tongue? The confidence our leader places in us should make us feel proud and satisfied.

KARK: I agree with you, Rick. Imagine, there are millions and millions of others, and only we have been selected to perform this staggering and risky mission.

KERK: Something more important must be taken into consideration, namely, that we are not from the old generation. On the contrary, we are the breed of the modern times.

MERK: Especially in this matter, we must admire the wisdom of our commander. His long experience tells him that the problems of our time require a new generation and new tactics to make people believe us and follow us. I think we should consider ourselves a highly-honored and privileged group because before us lies an urgent problem. On its success or failure depends the future of all mankind and his glory. No matter the price we pay, we must give him evidence that he can trust us.

RICK: (Standing up and thinking.) We are talking about our mission, but who among us has any idea of what we are expected to do?

MERK: Is it so much to ask? Up to the present moment, everything has been kept secret, and only three people have knowledge of it.

KARK: Merk, if you are one of them, you can tell us because I keep my mouth shut.

MERK:

Then keep your mouth shut now and do not ask me questions. One thing I know for sure that I can share with you is that when our leader is done exploring his mission, he will tell us. I think he will come very soon.

KERK:

(the youngest) I am sorry to interrupt you, but I must disagree. Why should we wait? Don't you realize that by waiting, we gain nothing and are wasting our time? Why don't we put our heads together and present our leader with our own strategy? Think about that!

MERK:

Maybe your enthusiasm deserves some applause, but we cannot accept it because our leader is on his highest mission. He is currently exploring the conditions we are to face shortly. At any moment he will be with us, so stay here and do not move.

Act I

Scene II The Leader Appears on the Scene.

ALL: Long live our leader! Long live our leader!

LEADER: Let me sit down and rest a bit because I am
                  exhausted.

KERK: We are anxious to hear you, to know your orders
                  for us. We cannot wait anymore, so tell us about
                  our next task.

LEADER: Do not lose patience. Keep still and listen to
                  me. I have been roaming these lands and have
                  discovered something very unusual and terrifying.
                  At the beginning of the world, the Creator
                  intended to establish His kingdom. I changed

his plans by using a cunning strategy with a woman who believed my flattering words and did what I invited her to do. From that moment, the intention of the Creator collapsed and vanished, and I established my own kingdom. However, now I have discovered that the Creator is awakening and has decided to put an end to our dominion over all the lands. Our domain is at stake. His plan is again associated with one woman. This time He has chosen a young girl, almost a child.

KARK: And why has He chosen a young girl instead of a mature woman? What kind of help can He expect from a stupid girl? That's ridiculous!

RICK: Why do you call it ridiculous? He probably does not trust a mature woman but harbors the illusion of better cooperation from an innocent but ignorant girl. Without realizing it, He is doing us a great favor. I would say He did not learn His lesson from the past, from His first mistake. Good for Him, but for us great joy!

MERK: That is fantastic. That He who calls himself infallible could overlook such a pregnant mistake. Let Him do whatever comes into His mind. That is His business, not ours.

KERK:

Let us put aside His business and instead think about our own. He is our leader; let him unfold his plan of operation.

LEADER:

The first woman wanted to know everything, the good and the evil. She aspired to become God Himself, but she went too far and burned her fingers. Our task is to obtain the contrary, to help the girl be very humble, to make her believe she is useless and good for nothing. Thus, she will reject God's plan because she will have profoundly accepted her inabilities.

KARK:

Excuse me, great leader, but who is this girl? May we know a bit about her?

LEADER:

Of course. It is absolutely necessary, and I will tell you without delay. Listen carefully. Roaming the lands, I came across a Nazarean woman. As a matter of fact, she is only a girl, almost a child, but more beautiful than the light of a spring day. I wanted to touch her, and an unknown force emanated from her. I lost my usual courage, and I recognized I could do nothing, so I left her alone.

RICK:

Leader, what you say seems impossible to believe and accept. I cannot imagine that one small girl could conquer our brave leader. That would be the most unimaginable humiliation in our long history.

MERK:

Comrades, I must speak in defense of our honor. Do we need a leader who is afraid of facing or touching a small girl? What could we expect of him if there were a need to confront the indomitable Cleopatra? Would you trust your life and honor to such a cowardly leader?

KERK:

I do not think we are here to criticize our leader without knowing the real motive for his bumbling. Let him stand his ground and defend himself.

LEADER:

Listen! You understand nothing about this subject. The girl, whom you ignore, found in the ancient books that God had a plan to restore His kingdom by sending a Messiah into the world. She is dreaming of becoming the mother of the Messiah.

She sounds like a simpleton, and although I do not pay much attention to her silly dreams, it is better to neither disdain her nor disregard her foolish beliefs.

KERK:

I utterly agree with our leader because I also know that some ancient people, called prophets, have been talking about the coming of an outstanding personality whom some call merely "Messiah," while others say his name is something like "Christ." Now, I ask you, what could the purpose of his coming be?

LEADER: His express purpose could be to destroy our kingdom and bring salvation to those oppressed in slavery,

MERK: And what about us? Will He save us as well?

RICK: You cannot argue with God. Our position is out of the question.

KERK: I suppose we overestimate the importance of the young girl because she cannot be the mother of the Messiah, being as penniless as she is. I presume that the Messiah will be the King of Israel, but the man who is living with the girl is a poor carpenter, a man without any high ambitions.

LEADER: No matter their real position, we cannot underestimate their importance. Doing so can leave us in a very critical situation.

KARK: How can we fight her when we do not know her name?

LEADER: Her name is Mary.

MERK: Mary! Oh, I am glad to hear that because she is my good friend. I have known her for several years. She is very active on the streets and is commonly known as a streetwalker.

LEADER:	I have no idea which Mary you have in mind. I think you are wrong because the Mary about whom I am talking is an innocent child and has nothing to do with living on the streets. Now, the most important thing is to sit down and study the plan we must put into practice very soon. We cannot fight directly against God. Instead, we must direct our energy against His plan to destroy our kingdom, which has existed since the Garden of Eden. I see two individuals who are very dangerous to us and who must be eliminated as soon as possible. One of them is a wild man who is preaching the coming of the new kingdom; his name is John. He is a dreamer. Less critical is another woman, but we cannot pass her by. Her dream is to become the wife of the king. We must help her achieve her ambition. Still, there remains one teenager who is very keen for money and who likes to dance for show.
KARK:	Leader, may I ask a question?
LEADER:	Of course, but be short and to the point. What is it?
KARK:	Should we kill those two women?
LEADER:	Of course not. We need them. They will be a fantastic help to us. Without them, our plan would not be feasible.

RICK: Leader, as I see it, your plan is already doomed to failure. How can you be so dumb, choosing two unqualified women instead of two men trained in diplomacy?

KARK: Insolent! How can you talk to our leader this way? You should immediately be thrown out from our group (grasps him by the neck and kicks him out).

LEADER: Hold it! This is no place for fighting. Remember the golden rule: If Satan expels Satan, his kingdom will be torn asunder. So, be quiet and listen to me. WE DECLARE WAR AGAINST THE CREATOR'S PLAN, AGAINST THOSE WHO DISAGREE WITH US.

ALL: Long Live our Leader! To war, to fight, to crush everyone who is opposed to us!

LEADER: I am proud of you. No power can resist us. Listen to my final words:

                    You, Rick, shorten the life of the wild man called John.

                    You, Merk, give an annulment to Philip and his wife and bring her to a new union with Herold.

                    You, Kark, the art of dance is your nature. Offer the first number to Herodias, in honor of the lustful king.

And now it is your turn, Rick. Your mission isn't easy; it is very delicate. You must persuade the little girl that her dream is evil and sinful. That the prophets are talking not about the coming of the Messiah, but about a king in the line of Solomon, one who will free their nation from Roman slavery, so she must be ready to serve in the king's court as a humble and faithful servant. Substitute her Bible for our bible.

Now, each of you go forward to occupy the most fitting and strategic places of observation. Use your brain, be courageous and without fear, and do not forget that you must decide, and assure us of our future: TO BE OR NOT TO BE.

ACT II

ACT II

Scene I. Shepherds Watching Their Flocks

Uncle, an old shepherd
Joshua and David, his sons
Jesse, the youngest son, a child

UNCLE: (looking around.) Hopefully, today will be much better than yesterday; it was like a small hurricane...

JESSE: Oh, I was terribly afraid that I would fly like a sparrow over the mountains, and then who would find me?

UNCLE:	I wish we could have a tranquil night and could rest without any new troubles because tomorrow we must move and look for a better place with green grass for our flock.
JOSHUA:	We deserve a good rest, and I think it is time to get under the tents.
DAVID	Strange but true! After yesterday's adventure, even our flocks keep quiet. There is no sign of a new storm, so I wish you a quiet and peaceful rest. Oh, no, no! We have forgotten to say goodbye to the Lord of our sheep.
JESSE:	You are entirely right; we have forgotten to read our Bible. Where is the Bible?
UNCLE:	You have to move your legs; it won't come by itself. Go fetch it.
DAVID:	Uncle, I do not understand why we should read the Bible every day. Don't you realize that the Bible is a very boring lecture? There is no fun in it, no laughing. Everything is very old-fashioned, relating to the history of the past. It says nothing about the future, forgetting to even mention some kind word about us poor shepherds.
JOSHUA:	I agree with David on everything because it is a sad truth. What interest do we have in remembering the dark pages of our history? Our life is gloomy enough without any prospect for a better and joyful tomorrow. Don't you see, Uncle,

that there is a big difference between you and us? You are an old man. What can we expect from your life? You move to your own end, while we are just beginning. We do not wish to continue our life under such hopeless conditions. Your day is made up of 24 hours, equal to the day of the sheep. We want to have a day of at least 26 hours, so we have two hours exclusively for our pleasure and continuing education.

DAVID: I completely support Joshua's ideas. For my part, I would suggest taking some sheep to the city and trading them for books and magazines of fiction, fantasy, and entertainment so we can experience more laughter, happiness, and joy. I do not see anything wrong with buying books of astrology so we can read the course of the stars every night. Who knows? Maybe we can learn the future of the world, and our future as well.

UNCLE: Ho, ho, ho! What crazy ideas are you harboring in your heads? Do you think that I find money on fake trees? I would be delighted if I could give you an education like King Solomon's, but...

JOSHUA: But what? If we cannot earn enough money working to make life more pleasant and useful, what is the purpose of wasting our youth in the service of animals?

JESSE:	(bringing the Bible) Finally, I got it. Touch it; it's still warm. One of the sheep was sleeping on it (passes it to Uncle).
UNCLE:	(smells it) You are right. I even know which one of the sheep was sleeping on it. I have been with them since childhood, and I know them better than my own pocket. I recognize them not only by their voice, but by their scent.
JESSE:	And what about you, Uncle? Do they recognize your smell?
UNCLE:	I do not have my own; what I have comes from a delicate and famous perfume made of roses. We are talking and forgetting the Bible (opening the Bible at random). What presents first will be first; here I have the prophet Ezekiel.
JESSE:	No, no! Who would listen to Ezekiel? It's too old a story. I would like to hear about the strong man who, with the jaw of a lion, killed 10,000 Philistines.
DAVID:	You'd better be quiet and listen to Uncle, who is known in this religion as the one most familiar with the Bible.
UNCLE:	Listen! Here I find something that excites my curiosity.

The Virgin shall be with child
and give birth to a son,
and shall call Him Emmanuel.

Curious! There must be something wrong
because a mother cannot be a virgin. That has
never happened in the history of mankind.
Maybe this is possible with a special kind
of monkey, but not with ordinary people.
Something must be wrong, or I do not know
how to interpret it.

JESSE: I think I know what the prophet wants to say.

UNCLE: Do you truly think you know?

JESSE: I think so. The prophet wants to say that the
child won't be a real child, but a toy.

ALL: (Laughing loudly)

JOSHUA: You are wiser than Solomon himself.

JESSE: And it makes you laugh? Why can't there be two
Solomons?

DAVID: Let Solomon aside. I have another question.
Uncle, you read in the book that a virgin will
bear a child who will be called Emmanuel. What
does Emmanuel mean? Does it mean the same as
Messiah?

UNCLE: It is hard to explain, but I will try to say it in a few words. By Messiah, we understand a man descended from David's line, who will occupy his throne and fight our enemies, free us from Roman domination, and make of us one universal kingdom. In other words, this world will belong to us. We will be the lords and the others will be slaves.

JESSE: That sounds marvelous. And I suppose we won't work anymore because the slaves will be working for us. Who knows? Instead of taking care of sheep, I may be put in charge of the royal court. Isn't that a fantastic idea?

JOSHUA: At what time will he come to us?

UNCLE: That is a good question, but almost impossible to answer because the prophet says nothing about the time period.

According to my calculations, it should be very soon. On the other hand, I am not much concerned about the time. What puzzles me is what we are to do with our sheep when the Messiah comes.

JESSE: Uncle, I do not see any problem. We can go to the Messiah, talk with Him, and propose a trade: You give us an excellent job in your kingdom, and we, in turn, will provide you with our sheep to help you feed your court. Will it happen to us before I become an old man?

UNCLE: Take a look at what the Bible says:

                I have made a covenant with my chosen one.
                I have sworn to David, my servant;
                Forever will I confirm your posterity
                And establish your throne for all generations.

JOSHUA: It means... The Bible wants to say that God
                promised to have on his throne someone of
                David's line who will fight the Romans and free
                us from their domination.

UNCLE: That is what we expect from him, one mighty
                Messiah to drive the Romans from our land.
                What time he will come, I cannot say. In truth,
                the prophet Isaiah says:

                For a child is born to us,
                A son is given to us.
                Upon his shoulders dominion rests.
                He will reign over David's throne

                And in another place, the Bible says:

                And you, Bethlehem, Land of Judah
                Are by no means least among the princes of
                Judah.
                Since from you shall come a ruler,
                Who is to shepherd my people Israel.

                At any rate, it is time to bring an end to our
                miserable occupation as shepherds and think
                about something better. Maybe this is the best

opportunity to try new business; otherwise, we might continue our life of serving sheep instead of serving the Messiah. I plan to sell our sheep, go to Jerusalem and wait for his coming (all are ready to move).

CHILD: Wait, wait! Do not move so quickly. Let me express my idea. I heard you saying that the mother of the Messiah is a poor woman. I suppose her son will also be a poor man. To help him, we can offer him our tents, which can help him start his new life.

DAVID: I must disagree with you because I think the Messiah would rather live close to the Pharisees and the royal court.

UNCLE: That is absolutely right; there is no doubt about it. Besides, the Bible says the Messiah will come from David's family, and David's family was not poor. They were wealthy people, so I am supporting David's idea. Anyway, we must think seriously about what we will do to welcome Him. Now, it is very late. Let us go to sleep and rest.

Act II

Scene II. The Annunciation. Room of Mary.

MARY: (sitting and reading the Bible).

The Lord says, Here is my servant, whom I
strengthen,
The one I have chosen, with whom I am pleased.
He will bring justice to every nation,
He will not shout, or raise his voice or make loud
speeches in the streets.
He will open the eyes of the blind, and set free
those
who sit in dark prisons.
He will be called WONDERFUL,
COUNSELOR, MIGHTY GOD,
PRINCE OF PEACE.

(closes the book and meditates.) From this passage, it seems to be clear that the Lord has a plan to send us someone special who would take care of the blind, of the prisoners, and reestablish peace.

MARY:

(reading the Bible).

In the sixth month, the angel Gabriel was sent from God to a town of Galilee named Nazareth, to a virgin. The virgin's name was Mary. Upon arriving, the angel said to her, Rejoice, O highly favored daughter.

(closes the Bible and asks herself.) Who might this virgin be, named Mary?

MARY

People are talking and talking, whether the subject is important or not, especially women; they cannot help spreading the pious and incredible news. I am a woman, as well, so why should I keep quiet? But I am afraid that my mother would scold me for harboring such extravagant ideas. Some people have gone so far as to say publicly that God will send an angel to a woman named Mary. I am only one of many others. Who can say that I am wrong in thinking of myself as the one whom God has elected? But I'm afraid such ideas can come only from the devil and not from God. I remember very well what my mother told me: When you are not sure about an important subject, always consult someone else before making a mistake. I am not sure whether that is true, but why not take a risk? Why should I allow another Mary the opportunity when I can take advantage of it myself?

MARIA: (her friend, a good talker, enters joyfully.) Hi Mary! You are alone. Why are you alone? If you don't mind, I would like to invite you to a small but lovely restaurant so I can introduce you to my friend. He is an exquisite boy. I am sure you will like him, and maybe he will like you. Of course, I'm not really sure, because you know how the boys of today are.

MARY: Must we go right now, or can we go a little bit later?

MARIA: Right now! I am very much in a hurry.

MARY: As usual. You are always in a hurry; you never have time for me or even for yourself.

MARIA: And what do you expect from me? I am interested in many things, so I have no time to waste. Tell me, what is your new problem today?

MARY: It's not a new problem. It is a problem of yesterday and any other day. I did not say I won't go. The only favor I would like to ask is that you stay with me for a short while. We can discuss a problem I found in the Bible.

MARIA: Don't talk to me about the Bible. I am sick and tired of listening to your stories from the Bible. Don't you have any interest in better books? If you wish, I can go with you to any store where we can get books about every pleasure.

MARY: Maria, why are you so excitable today? Did you get out of bed on the wrong side? Can't you spend a few minutes with me today?

MARIA: OK. What is your problem? Tell me right now.

MARY: While reading the Bible today, I had the impression that it is talking about us. Look at verse 16.

MARIA: Mary, pardon me, but that is not to my interest. Leave the Book and let's go see my new friend. He is a charming boy, as I said. I am sure you will love him at first glance.

MARY: Maria, I am grateful for your concern for me, but maybe...

MARIA: What do you mean by maybe? There is no time for maybe. What you need to learn is to take your life into your own hands.

MARY: That is precisely what I am doing. I am taking my life into my hands.

MARIA: Don't be silly. You have no idea what it means to live, or how to spend the most beautiful time of a girl's life. We are young and it is our time. We must enjoy the best of it; otherwise, before long, you will be a grandma.

MARY: OK, Maria. I'll do you a favor, but before I do, you do one for me. How about that?

MARIA: Not a bad idea; I accept.

MARY: In reading the Bible, I found one sentence I do not understand. As bright as you are, maybe you can help me understand it. I even suspect that the Bible is talking about you.

MARIA: Don't be silly. About me? That is absolutely impossible.

MARY: OK. Let's take a look.

In the sixth month, the angel Gabriel was sent from God to a town of Galilee named Nazareth to a virgin named Mary.

What do you think about it? Pay attention! The angel is talking about our city, Nazareth, about a woman who is a virgin, and whose name is Mary. Don't you think he is talking about us, you and me? Our names are one and the same, although they sound different.

MARIA: Maybe you are right, but not totally. I imagine that when God sends His angel, He sends him on a great mission. According to that, He is looking for a wise and favorite girl whom He can trust and rely on to achieve His plan. In such a case, I am sorry to say, He could not be thinking of you.

MARY: Maybe you are right. We are different personalities

MARIA: That is precisely the reason why I said He could not be thinking about you. I am sure God is looking for a more mature girl who knows about life and how to have a good time. And you? What do you do? You spend all your time reading the Bible and going to the temple. The Bible won't tell you what life is about, how to enjoy it, how to tackle its problems. The practical knowledge of this thing you cannot learn from the Bible but from your daily contact with people and their problems.

MARY: I understand, and I give you credit for being much better prepared than I am for any visit of an angel from heaven.

MARIA: Thank you, Mary, for saying this. I was afraid of offending and hurting you. Without boasting, I am much better prepared to perform a mission of God than you are, if that were the will of God.

MARY:

Very well said -- if that were the will of God. You can help God as a great employee. On the other hand, I might be a mere servant in His hands.

MARIA:

I hope you realize, Mary, that God has no need for useless servants. As you evaluate yourself, you might be useful in peeling the potatoes for the royal kitchen. Wouldn't you like to do that?

MARY:

If that would be the will of God, yes. It might be challenging to spend my life peeling potatoes, but I would not protest. I would act according to His will.

MARIA:

I am sorry to hear that. I think we have nothing more to say. You serve Him as His faithful servant, and I will wait for a sign of His will, to serve him.

One more thing, Mary. Promise me, as I promise you, that if an angel comes to you first, you will let me know about it, and if he comes to me first, I will let you know about it. Do you promise and agree that all this must be kept in strict secret?

MARY:

I don't think that will be necessary because if that happens, you will know sooner or later, in one way or another. Shalom, Maria (Maria leaves the room).

Act II

Scene III. Azazel, an Old Man, Dressed Like a Pharisee.

AZAZEL: And yet, God is faithful to his words. A long time ago, he spoke through the prophets that He would send us a Messiah who would free us from the Roman power. It seems the time has already come.

AHAB: Master, why do you say that? Have you heard anything about his coming?

AZAZEL: If what people are saying is true, the Messiah should be a historical fact.

AHAB: Master, people are always saying things, but seldom are they accurate.

AZAZEL: Of course, you cannot take for granted what people are saying. I know that very well, but this time the whole story seems to be different. People say that an angel of the Lord had been sent to a girl named Mary, and she had a special baby who one day will occupy the throne of David. The girl was said to be betrothed to a man named Joseph, who is a descendant of King David.

AHAB: Mary! Mary! I think I know her, and I remember she was a beautiful girl.

AZAZEL: And the story goes on that an angel came to her and said:

Peace be with you, Mary;
The Lord is with you.
You are greatly blessed.

AHAB: Did Mary understand the angel's message?

AZAZEL: I doubt it very much. I am sure she was terrified when she suddenly saw an overpowering angel in her room, telling her such incredible news. One thing is sure — she was very troubled by the angel's message and wondered what his words meant.

AHAB: To tell the truth, I am delighted that the angel came not to me, but to her because I would have been scared, consumed, to the bottom of my heart!

AZAZEL: The best proof that she was afraid is the reaction of the angel. When he saw that Mary was afraid, he immediately came to her help and said:

Do not be afraid, Mary.
God has been gracious to you.
You will give birth to a son,
And you will name him Jesus.

Ahab, do you know how old this girl is?

AHAB: I am sorry, but I do not know her exact age. She must be very young, seeing that the Bible says she is still a virgin.

AZAZEL: That is what puzzles me. I cannot imagine a girl both virgin and pregnant. I suppose her husband must be a man of advanced age, or maybe she even pretends to say she is pregnant without a husband.

AZAZEL: Please do not misunderstand me. I like women, but I have always had many problems with them. It is nice to have a woman, but sometimes it would be better to live without one.

AHAB: You should have known that before your marriage, not now. That is your problem and not mine. Turning back to your topic, do you know the husband of that young girl?

AZAZEL: I do not know him, but I think we have a solution. Listen to what the Bible says about this event. The angel told her:

The Holy Spirit will come upon you,
And God's power will rest upon you.

AHAB:

That makes sense; now I see. But one thing
bothers me — how people learn about those
things which should remain a strict secret.
The visit of the angel undoubtedly was private
business, and probably no one knew about it.

AZAZEL:

I try to understand it straightforwardly. The young
girl, overwhelmed with happiness, could not help
herself and ran immediately to her kinswoman
Elizabeth, telling her the whole story. From that
moment, the private secret became the public
secret. You know very well that the best way to
broadcast a secret is to tell it to a woman. The angel
said not only that Mary would become pregnant
but also that her cousin Elizabeth was already
pregnant. Unfortunately, my wife is no exception.
She is a perfect tool for spreading a secret. I
learned a good lesson from her: When you wish to
keep a secret, never tell a woman to please promise
to keep her mouth shut. I always say that it is not
essential, or I say it without restrictions; then the
secret never returns to me as a secret.

AHAB:

Thank you for that. In life, there is always
something to learn.

ACT III

ACT III

Scene I. A Child Is Born

	Holy Family abode. Mary is dusting some furniture.
JOSEPH:	Good morning, Mary. How do you feel today?
MARY:	Pretty well. There is no particular reason for the change, at least for the moment.
JOSEPH:	I am afraid to say that your feelings may be misguiding you today.
MARY:	Is something wrong? Has something happened to you?

JOSEPH: Listen! What has happened may not be wrong
             but simply hard to accept because it was
             unexpected.

MARY: Do you think so? What can happen to us? We are
             in the hands of God; he will protect us.

JOSEPH: That is very true. I know that God won't leave
             us alone, but there are two different worlds:
             what God disposes of and what man eliminates.
             These two worlds do not always work in perfect
             harmony, and we must depend on both of them.

MARY: Do not worry. No one is more powerful than
             God.

JOSEPH: Yes, I know. God has infinite power, and he
             seldom uses it to destroy minor forces that stand
             in his way.

MARY: In this, we have no problem, but tell me, what
             bothers you?

JOSEPH: The bad news is that Caesar Augustus has issued
             a decree that a census should be taken of the
             entire Roman empire. We must get ready to go to
             Bethlehem, the town of David.

MARY: That is unusual and not very easy in our
             situation. When must we leave Nazareth?

JOSEPH: The sooner, the better. Take only essential items; the rest we will ask our kind neighbors and God to take care of. While you make the necessary preparations, I will prepare our faithful donkey. Without it, we could not undertake such a long and fatiguing journey. (leaving)

MARY: (stays, thinking, one hand touching in front of her)

JOSEPH: Any problems? Are you afraid?

MARY: No, I am not afraid of the road, but you know that the baby is on the way. It can happen any day and then what do we do? We don't have relatives there.

JOSEPH: Let us put it all into the hands of God. He will provide what we need and what we cannot do ourselves. (leaves her)

MARY: (praying)

Hearken to my words, O Lord,
Attend to my sighing.
Heed my call for help,
My King and my God!
To you I pray, O Lord;
At dawn you hear my voice;
At dawn I bring my plea expectantly before you.

JOSEPH: (looking around) We have so little, and even that we must leave.

MARY: It is an unfortunate place, but we were always under a roof and now?

JOSEPH: Don't worry, Mary, we can stand up to anything that comes.

Act III

Scene II Mary and Joseph on their Journey to Bethlehem

NARRATOR:
With an encouraging look at Mary, Joseph helps his wife mount the donkey and says, "Let's go." The road is not easy but neither is it especially dangerous because they are not alone. Hundreds of people of the city of Bethlehem are moving with them.

Joseph, a healthy young man, measured the distance between cities on foot, while Mary, mounted on their faithful companion, did not realize what was happening around her. Her mind was on the event that was fast approaching. Joseph was tired and thirsty, but not broken. He looked at the city while the sun changed its golden color to red. At that moment, a question filled his mind: Will I find a comfortable place for my wife? The multitude of rich people and the many caravans moving on the streets of Bethlehem seemed to tell him: Who am I and who is my poor donkey to open the hearts of those who expect to make a good business from all these visitors?

Hoping for the best, he dared knock on the first door, asking: "Do you have a small room for my wife and me?" A negative response forced Joseph to move from door to door. Everywhere, he heard, "I see you are here for the census, too. People have been coming all day, and every room is filled." To better make the innkeeper understand his predicament, Joseph said, "Sir, my wife is going to have a baby; do you not have even one small place?" "I told you," the innkeeper said, "I don't have any more room. Now, go away and do not bother me." "Sir," said Joseph, "Did I command Caesar to proclaim a census? Am I responsible for Rome's demand to drag honest people from their homes to the towns of their birth so they could be counted?" "Well, there is a cave you can use, a stable where the animals are kept," the innkeeper said. "Joseph replied respectfully, "Thank you, sir" (Mary and Joseph move toward the cave).

Song: O Little Town of Bethlehem.

Act III

Scene III Shepherds Watching Their Flocks.

Dark and still. Tents, a fireplace, people sleeping in tents; a dog barking several times.

CHILD: Be quiet, Moshel; don't you know it is night? Lie down and sleep; be quiet (dog barking, again). Don't you understand me? Be quiet (red light on one side; dog continues to bark). Father, father, wake up!

FATHER: What is going on? Why don't you sleep?

CHILD: There must be something wrong because Moshel keeps barking. There must be wild beasts.

FATHER: Yeah, yeah, I hear him barking, but I don't believe there is anything wrong. But what light is there? Do you see it?

CHILD: A red color, like blood. What does it mean?

FATHER: (Gets up.) There must be something going on. I am afraid our town is on fire. Boys, boys, get up quickly! Bethlehem is on fire! Move! Move!

SHEPHERDS: (Rubbing their eyes.) What is going on? Why are you so noisy?

ASA: Who would want to burn our city?

FATHER: Don't ask stupid questions. Get up! Run for your life! Horrible! It seems the whole city is on fire, and who knows what will happen to our poor homes and families? Let's get out now and save our families. (Stands in a position to run away.)

(Change of light to natural. The voice of an angel.)

FATHER: Wait a moment. I hear a voice.

AMMON: A voice coming from over there. Look at... (Song of angels.)

ANGEL: Don't be afraid. I bring you good news of great joy that will be for all people. Today in the town of David, a Savior has been born to you. He is Christ the Lord. This will be a sign to you. You will find a baby wrapped in swaddling clothes and lying in a manger. Go and admire Him! (The light dims slowly; the angel disappears.)

FATHER:	Can what we heard be true? Are we dreaming?
ABEL:	How can we know? We must go and see with our own eyes.
ASHER:	Why are we waiting? Hurry!
FATHER:	It's all right. We will go and adore Him, but not in such a hurry. We must be sure about the place where he was born. It is time for reflection. If what the angel said is true, it means the child was born in a cave. His mother must be an impoverished woman, without a home, so the child is also poor. We cannot go there with empty hands. We must help the child and his mother. We are poor people too, but they seem to be even poorer. We must help them.
ASA:	Yes, we should help them, but do we know what they really need?
FATHER:	We know they are poor, and they need what poor people need -- something to eat and wear. That is about all we can offer them. Now, get together and think about what we can take with us.
CHILD:	I will take my flute. Maybe the child will one day become a shepherd. He will not only talk to his flock, but entertain them with beautiful music.
ASHER:	I will take a few sheep felts so the child can sleep with comfort and be protected against the cold. Even his parents will have no need to sleep on the floor.

ASA: I am thinking about giving the whole family something to eat. I hope they wouldn't reject a good lump of cheese. Of course, I will take fresh cheese so the child can have some as well.

FATHER: They cannot live on cheese alone, so I will take the fattest sheep to give the family fresh milk. We are poor shepherds, so we cannot give them luxuries.

AMMON: Father, I have nothing to offer, but I am thinking of offering myself. Would that be ok?

FATHER: It most certainly would be. Your gift may be the most appreciated of all.

ACHAN: The cave has no light, so I will take them a lamp with matches. I think that is good, don't you?

FATHER: That is a great idea, and it will help them every night.

ABEL: You forget the most essential piece of clothing a baby needs -- a diaper. I still have a brand-new set. I kept it for a special occasion, and this is the most supreme occasion.

FATHER: What more do we need? We are not rich and we can offer nothing better. We can ask them to tell us their most urgent need, and if it is not too much, we can furnish it. Now, get ready to go to Bethlehem and take whatever you plan to offer.

Act III

Scene IV. Nearing Bethlehem

> The shepherds travel joyfully toward the city.
> Suddenly, a group of devils approaches them.
> They are dressed elegantly and in uniform. They
> great them politely.

FIRST DEVIL: Friends, where are you going? Reading your tired faces, I suppose you are on a long journey.

FATHER: Thank you for your kindness. We are not coming from across the road. We feel tired because the path is not covered with roses, but with stones and thorns.

FIRST DEVIL: I get the impression that you are searching for someone or something.

FATHER: You must be a smart person to read that in our faces. We are not going for a picnic, but to find someone significant.

FIRST DEVIL: No matter the reason for your journey to Bethlehem, I must tell you, as a good friend, that you will find yourselves in a very unpleasant situation. Turn back and do not go there.

SECOND DEVIL: We are returning from Bethlehem because there is no place to sleep. Don't you know about the decree of Caesar?

FATHER: Nothing. Is there bad news?

THIRD DEVIL: You'd better listen to what we tell you. The absence of any accommodations is not even the worst! There is nothing to eat, nothing to drink, and not because of the thousands of visitors, but because of the selfishness of the people. To save you any unpleasantness, we advise you to turn back and go home. I am telling you, as you are the leader responsible for the welfare of your group. Would you like to go to hell?

FATHER: What a devilish question! Who would like to go to hell? As far as I know, hell is the worst place you can imagine.

FIRST DEVIL: Maybe you are right, but I am not entirely sure. Unfortunately, that is the horrible picture visitors have of the once beautiful and peaceful city of

Bethlehem. You cannot take two steps forward and one backward without hearing people. Sir, if you are honest people, turn back on the spot and go home.

FATHER: (turning toward the group.) What is your opinion? I think we must be grateful to this gentleman for his concern about our souls.

ASA: It is hard to believe such incredible things could happen in only a few days.

FIRST DEVIL: Sir, you know that today there are no miracles, only lies.

FOURTH DEVIL: You have no choice; the only possible option is no choice.

FIFTH DEVIL: I must tell you, you would painfully regret obeying only the voice of your conscience. Would you like to be victims of your own foolishness? Do not make a foolish decision today. Tomorrow may be too late.

AMMON: (looking at his father.) I cannot believe you would like to lead us to a place of perdition and corruption.

FATHER: God condemn me if I would be so perverted. There is no time to think, but a crucial opportunity to act. Let us return to our flock (they turn back and start to move).

Meanwhile, the devils say, "Go, go to your sheep and good luck to you," grimacing and watching them leave.

While the shepherds are turning back, a bright light shines, and a song is heard:

Glory to God in the Highest.

Upon hearing the song, both groups stop and remain immobile.

SHEPHERDS:	What is that? (They stay, listening to the song.)
DEVILS:	The heavens are open; the powers of Heaven are against us. Let's get away!
ABEL:	Look, those gentlemen are running away. They have tails. They cannot be human beings; human beings have no tails.
AMMON:	Then what are they? They must be ghosts or devils that intended to cheat us, to stop us from going to Bethlehem.
ASA:	To hell with them; to hell forever.
ACHAN:	Oh, we were so stupid. We honored them as great gentlemen when they were ordinary devils.

FATHER: We are to blame for being so gullible. Why did none of us recognize them for what they were? The devils have returned to their proper place, so now let's go to Bethlehem. As the angel said to us with courage, have no fear! Go to Bethlehem, where the Messiah is born to you. Let's go quickly because I am afraid the devils will get there before we do and steal or adore the baby.

ASA: What? Devils adore the infant child? Who told you such a silly story?

FATHER: Maybe not to adore the baby, but to see it. It would be a shame if they arrived before us, so let's go.

ACT III

Scene V

The shepherds travel to the cave, where they find a baby in a crib. They kneel and look toward the cradle.

A choir of angels appears, singing:
Glory to God in the highest, and on earth,
Peace to men of good will.

ANGEL: Glory to God who has descended from heaven and taken on mortal flesh from the Virgin. Glory to God that tonight, He was born in a poor and humble stable.

CHOIR:	Glory to God... (little by little, the light dims and the angels disappear).
ASA:	What a marvelous choir of angels.
ACHAN:	How happy God must be, listening every day to the music of those beautiful angels.
AMMON:	And imagine how our life would change if God were to send us one angel every day to sing one celestial song, instead of our listening to the bleating of our sheep.
ACHAN:	Yes, our lives would take on a new color. Unfortunately, we were born shepherds and will probably end our lives as shepherds.
	Song (they kneel in a circle).
ABEL:	(gets up and goes to Mary). Gracious Lady, we are poor and uneducated shepherds; we come to visit you and your baby. I do not know your name. Would it be too much to ask? Would you do me this favor?
MARY:	With great pleasure. My name is Mary, and I am the mother of the child you came to adore.
ABEL:	You are a beautiful lady, and I hope you are pleased as the mother of this child.
MARY:	You are right, I can assure you. There cannot be any higher happiness than His life.

ABEL:

I wish I could have a mother like you, but that is impossible. My mother is a very poor woman.

MARY:

Be cheerful. The time will come when you will be very happy in this life.

ABEL:

Do you really mean that? Thank you, I will try to remember you.

MARY:

May I ask your name?

ABEL:

Oh, my name is very famous because it was the name of the second son of Eve, and I am also the second son of my mother. My father is here; come, Father, over here.

FATHER:

Beautiful lady, we are poor people. We take care of animals in the fields.

ABEL:

Father, let me continue my story, if you please.

MARY:

Of course, your story is not only yours but a story of my son. I assure you that from now on, whenever people talk about my son, they will also talk about you. Isn't that wonderful?

ABEL:

You mean, we will become great and famous one day?

MARY:

Exactly!

ABEL:

Father, did you hear what the lady is telling us?

FATHER: Hm, hm. Pardon me, but it's hard to believe that from one miserable shepherd I could become known all over the world.

MARY: It is true.

ABEL: Lady, you don't know how much I love you for being so kind to me and showing me that I can still become a famous person, even as a poor shepherd. Thank you. Now I see I won't die like a sheep but like a person. Before I leave, I would like to sing to your baby. Would you mind if I do so?

MARY: It would give me great pleasure.

ASHER: Abel, do not think only of yourself; we would like to sing to the baby also (all get up and go to the crib).

ACHAN: The baby is sleeping, so we can sing a soft lullaby without waking him.

Song   O Lulajze Jesuni.

The offering of gifts by the shepherds.

FATHER: Lady, we are poor, but at least we have our own tents. You are more impoverished, living in an animal shelter, so we come to offer your baby (you must accept potluck!) our best goat, which will provide enough milk for your family. I am very sorry I cannot offer something better. These are my own shoes...

ABEL:	Since this is your birthday and I have no birthday cake, I would like to substitute a lump of cheese, so your baby will never go to bed hungry.
ASA:	In this part of the country, the winter is not always agreeable. The nights are cold, so to protect your child from the inclement weather, there is nothing better than warm sheep leather. He can grow healthy and stay immune from sickness.
ACHAN:	I don't know whether your child will be an exception, but as far as I know, all children make trouble for every mother. To make your care more comfortable, I offer two pairs of diapers.
AMMON:	Lady, your child is born in very humble conditions, in a stable, but I hope you will soon move to a big city like Jerusalem, where he can avoid ridicule. I offer him a T-shirt so he can feel comfortable in the company of his peers.
FATHER:	Son, you have forgotten that one who offers diapers and sheets must also provide a washing machine. Without a washing machine, your gift is not very helpful.
AMMON:	What should I do?
JOSEPH:	Son, do not worry about it. I am a good carpenter, and I can make a brand-new washing machine without wasting one cent.

AMMON: Can you? Will it work?

JOSEPH: That is another question; I cannot guarantee it.

AMMON: That is your problem. If it doesn't work, do not
                 blame me; send it to the Blessed Sacrament
                 auction.

JOSEPH: Oh, I won't. Instead, I am grateful for the very
                 useful presents you have brought our little baby
                 (they withdraw to one side).

ACT IV

ACT IV

Scene I.

(Enter a group of small girls, opposite.)

NAOMI: Little baby, sleeping in the hay. This Christmas morning is your birthday. With shepherds on the hillside and angels in the air, we wish you a delightful day. Although we are little, we want to show our love for you.

REBECCA: My mother calls me Rebecca. I came to worship your little baby and to offer him my praises. I do not know how to pray, but I know how to love. Receive my little heart and make it grow as big as your own.

SARA:

My mother calls me Sara because I was born when she was very old. I am here to bring you my gift of time. I help my mother every day. I dust and run the sweeper before I go out to play.

RUTH:

My name is Ruth. Everybody who reads the Bible knows how sweet my name is. I bring my gift of love. I try to obey and never cause my family trouble by wanting to have my own way.

MIRIAM:

I hope, little baby, that one day you will love my gift of joy, of happiness, and of cheer. I wish it would be yours not only during the Christmas season but throughout the whole new year.

MARY:

The angels praise my Son in Heaven, and shepherds praise my child on earth. All of you honor Him with all the power of your hearts. I thank you for the beautiful love you have shown to my child lying in the hay.

ALL TOGETHER

(bowing their heads):

Goodbye, beautiful Mother. Goodbye, beautiful child. (One of them.) This was the happiest day of our lives. We wish to serve you, and when the time comes for you to sit on the throne of David in Jerusalem, remember us.

MARY

You will always be remembered. Good times will come for you (they leave the scene).

(Enter another group of children.)

FIRST CHILD:	Dear God, we thank you for your Son
	Who came to earth a little one,
	Who lived to teach us how we should
	Be to all people; kind and pleasant.
SECOND CHILD:	We honor Him with speech and song
	Our songs and praise to Him belong;
	With joyful hearts, we bow and say
	A prayer of thanks for Christmas Day.
THIRD CHILD:	You are a special child
	Whose lowly, humble birth
	Will change the course of mankind
	Who live on planet Earth
FOURTH CHILD:	He was born in a town
	That was not big in size
	The town of Bethlehem
	Was special in God's eyes.
FIFTH CHILD:	He was a special child
	Who came to change the course
	So mankind could be saved
	From Satan's deadly force.
	(Enter a group of shepherds, ringing bells.)
JOSHUA:	I just love a Christmas bell
	It tells of the love and joy
	That came that night in Bethlehem
	With the birth of a baby boy (ring).

DAVID: That baby was Jesus
                   Ring out each pretty bell
                   For you have a unique story
                   That you are supposed to tell.

JESSE: Ring, ring, pretty bells
                   Ring tidings across the earth
                   Ring out the blessed story
                   It is the day of Jesus' birth (ring)

UNCLE: Christmas is a wonderful time
                   With exceptional sounds and joys;
                   Happy times for everyone
                   For little girls and boys.

                   Singing: Silent Night.

ACT IV

Scene II. The Magi Visit Herod

	An officer reports the arrival of the Three Kings to Herod.

OFFICER: Your Majesty, three tourists are asking for an audience with you.

HEROD: Three tourists? Who are they?

OFFICER: They say they are kings of the East. They humbly ask for an audience with Your Majesty.

HEROD: Three tourists from afar! What do they say about themselves? Are they vagabonds?

OFFICER: I am sorry, I cannot answer Your Majesty's questions. It is the first time they have visited your kingdom. They seem to be very peaceful people. They are dressed in Oriental style.

HEROD: Keep your eyes open, and let them come in.

OFFICER: (bows to the king and goes to the three tourists, announcing the good news). Gentlemen, my King and my Lord is pleased to welcome you into his throne room. Please... (invites the three tourists and goes ahead of them).

BALTHAZAR: Oh, great King of the Jews, we are very grateful for your kindness and interest in helping us. We are kings, but our people call us wise men because we spend our lives searching for the truth. Recently, we have heard about the birth of a new Jewish king.

HEROD: What? Can you repeat that? Maybe I didn't hear you correctly or misunderstood your words.

BALTHAZAR: Excuse me, Your Majesty; I am sorry I did not express myself correctly.

HEROD: Do not worry. That can happen to any of us, to a king and to a wise man. Please continue your story. It is fascinating, and I depend on your words.

BALTHAZAR: As I said, we, meaning me and my companions, come to worship the newly born king of Jerusalem.

HEROD:	Ha! Of Jerusalem? That is a pretty story, but I am surprised to hear this from wise men from afar and not from my religious leaders. Maybe I am too naive, believing in their loyalty while they plot against me. Poor slaves; they forget who I am and what I can do to them.
BALTHAZAR:	Your Majesty, let me continue my story, if you don't mind.
HEROD:	Before I use my power, I want you to know that I am Herod, the mighty king of the Jews, and I will use every effort to help you. I would be pleased to accompany you to that place, but as you well know, no king is a free person in his kingdom. I must stay here and keep an eye on everything that is happening. I am willing to cooperate with you on the condition that you work with me (rings bell and one officer enters).
OFFICER:	To serve Your Majesty.
HEROD:	Go tell the high priest to gather the chief priests and scribes of the people. Order them to find the answer to the question of these honorable wise men from the East: Where is the Messiah to be born? Report to me without delay.
OFFICER:	In the service of Your Majesty, always (greets Herod and backs off).

HEROD: (to the three wise men). My people are politically rebellious but religiously devoted to their God, Yahweh. They continually await the coming of some unknown Messiah. No one knows who this strange personality is, but the Jews believe he will come to destroy the Roman Empire. Poor, blind people; they ignore the fact that no power on earth can conquer the Roman Legions. I am sure you will have your answer at any moment. Our Jewish leaders know their book as I know my kingdom.

OFFICER: (announces the coming of the high priest).

HIGH PRIEST: Your Majesty! Your servant is happy to bring you good news. We have found the place of the birth of the Messiah. The great prophet Micah says very clearly:

And you, Bethlehem of Judah, are by no means least among the princes of Judah
Since from you shall come a ruler
Who is to shepherd my people Israel.

HEROD: Thank you for your service. Well done (high priest leaves the room). (addresses the Wise Men.) My friends, I announce to you good news. This is the happiest day of my reign in Jerusalem. I am a king of many troubles and heartaches. As a man of advanced age and childless, I was looking for a successor, and the solutions come when least expected. My dream has been fulfilled. And now, my good friends, go to Bethlehem and get detailed information about the child. When you have found him, do not delay in reporting it to me, so my court and I may also go and offer him homage.

CASPAR: Your Majesty, now we understand the meaning of the star that guided us to you. Heaven has chosen you as a means to spread the news of the coming of the Messiah. We wish that your gods will guide you to your personal happiness and fulfillment (they leave the presence of the king).

ACT IV

Scene III. Home of Mary, Joseph, Child

The three wise men are traveling toward Bethlehem.

NARRATOR: When Jesus was born in Bethlehem of Judea in the days of Herod, the king, behold, there came wise men from the East to Jerusalem, asking for the newborn king of the Jews. Being instructed about the place by King Herod, they came to the site with great joy. When they went into the house, they saw the young child with Mary, his mother, and Joseph, and they fell down and worshipped Him; and when they opened their treasures, they presented unto Him gifts.

Song: Three Kings of the Orient.

NARRATOR: (carrying a star on a pole).
                         Three Wise men living in the East
                         Traveled from afar,
                         Going down to Bethlehem
                         Guided by a star.

                         On coming to the house, they saw the child
                         with his mother, Mary,
                         And they bowed down and worshiped Him.
                         Then they opened their treasures and presented
                         Him with gifts of gold and incense and myrrh.

MELCHIOR: (carrying a golden box.)
                         Gold I bring to offer you
                         Messiah, the newborn King
                         A worthy gift for one so small
                         Of whom the angels sing.

BALTHAZAR: (carrying an incense burner.)
                         Frankincense to offer I have.
                         It burns with sweet delight,
                         A priceless gift for God's own son
                         Born on that Christmas night.

CASPAR: (carrying a purple box.)
                         No better perfume can be found
                         Than myrrh I also bring
                         To offer to the promised one
                         Who is the King of kings.

JOSEPH: I am a simple man, getting bread for our daily living with my two hands. For your generosity, I thank you heartily. Looking at your gifts, I am wondering what use to make of the gold you have offered us. Maybe it will buy a suitable house for the baby and his mother and a workshop for me.

MARY: Looking at you three wise men from afar, curiosity crossed my mind. How did you discover the bright star, and how did you learn to read the message it brought you? Did someone tell you about it, or did you come to the knowledge by accident, or even through divine revelation?

MELCHIOR: If I said no one, I would be lying. If I said someone, I would not know who he was. I prefer to say that He who made the world also knew how to communicate this marvelous news of the coming of the Messiah.

MARY: I think that He who knows how to create things also finds appropriate means to spread the news about them.

MELCHIOR: Each night, for many years, I have studied the stars, but nothing like this has happened to me before. Never have I seen a star so bright. I suspected that heaven had a special message for me. In the ancient book, the coming of a savior

	to help us is written. I took the brilliant light as a sign of heaven calling me.
CASPAR:	Today, overjoyed with happiness, we have found the truth for which we have searched many years.
Song:	Hark, the Herald Angels Sing.
NARRATOR:	And it happened that, in a dream, they received a message to not return to Herod, so they went back to their own country by another route.

END

NARRATOR: We hope you have appreciated and enjoyed our presentation of The Nativity of Jesus. Happy birthday, Dear Jesus, happy birthday to you, and Happy New Year as well. May the coming holidays be filled with peace and cheer and may the days of Christmas be yours all through the year.

This simple presentation is telling you that baby Jesus, God's only Son, was born on Christmas Day. If every day were Christmas, how different life would be. If not one day but every day of the year were ruled by charity and love, we would learn not how to get but only how to give.

Happy Birthday, baby Jesus, today we come to honor you. Happy birthday, baby Jesus, our joy is real because of you. Because God so loved the world that he gave his only Son, that whoever believes in Him shall not perish but have Eternal Life.

Song: We Wish You a Happy Christmas.

A Brief Biography of
Father Chester Fabisiak, SJ

Father Chester Fabisiak, SJ, was born on **June 11, 1911,** in Poznan, Poland.

On June 18, 1911, he was baptized into Christ.

In **1927,** he entered the Society of Jesus, and in **1939,** he was ordained a priest.

In **1939,** he was taken a prisoner by Nazi SS commandos.

April 29, 1945, he was liberated by Allied forces from Dachau Nazi concentration camp near Munich.

After liberation, he served more than 20 years as a missionary in South America, primarily in Bolivia, Venezuela, and Ecuador.

He completed his final 30 years of the missionary devotion in the United States.

He proudly became a U.S. citizen. The everlasting gratitude he held in his heart was expressed daily by helping men, women, and the future generation by teaching the children and teenagers whom he loved.

From **1966 to 1969,** he served in New York City.
From **1969 to 1974,** he served in Michigan.

In **1974,** he came to the Springfield Diocese, serving the parishes of Saints Peter and Paul, St. Mary, Taylorville, St. Mary, New Berlin, and St. Boniface, Quincy.

From **1981** until his death, he lovingly served at Blessed Sacrament Parish, Springfield, Illinois.

With God's grace, Father Fabisiak was able to provide his services to the last day of his life.

Some of the highlights of his ministries at Blessed Sacrament included celebrating the early- morning Mass at 6:20 AM, ministering to the elderly in local high-rises, and making his services unrestrictedly available to all in need, which was his joy-but preparing children for the Godly, spiritual life was his passion.

December 9, 1996, Father Chester Fabisiak, SJ.

At rest with God on the Feast of the Immaculate Conception.

Upcoming Publications

Please watch for the upcoming publication of *Memories of a Devil,* also by Father Chester Fabisiak, SJ. It is his journal from Dachau, the Nazi concentration camp.

His memoir of life as a young Jesuit priest will take you not only through the atrocities of the Nazi concentration camp but also through a much more in-depth encounter with God, evil, and humanity challenged by those powerful forces.

44607806R00055

Made in the USA
Columbia, SC
19 December 2018